Sabbaticals and Freelancing

Exploring Options to the Great Resignation

Julia Durand
Bridgeway 36 Inc.

Forward

Over the course of 2021, more than 47 million people quit their jobs, representing 23% of the total U.S. workforce, according to the Bureau of Labor Statistics (BLS). And in 2022, roughly 38 million more quit.

The Great Resignation, which began around April 2021, has seen more than four million US workers quitting their jobs every month. While numbers began to tick down slightly in September 2022, the latest data from the US Bureau of Labor Statistics showed 4.17 million people quit their jobs in November 2022.

Employees quit their jobs over the past two years for five main reasons:

- They were doing the workload of a fully staffed team with fewer team members.

- They needed better work-life balance brought on by pandemic pressures and new lifestyles.

- They had new job opportunities in the same or different fields.

- There were opportunities to be self-employed, start a new business, or become a gig worker.

- Their proximity to retirement and a reluctance to shift to new ways of working prompted them to retire early.

The continued turnover of employees — despite concerns of a looming recession and high inflation point to many signs as the various findings indicate. Employees are seeking greater freedom, work life balance and opportunity for growth.

Many enjoyed the remote work environment and are seeking employers who continue to offer remote working.

As employers continue to seek ways to attract and retain employees, as noted in my book Bridgeway to Business Real Solutions for the Un-employed and over 50, "By the year 2040 fifty percent of the population will be age 50+, they will need us! Get Ready". What if employees like their job and what they are doing but just need a break?

Many of those who resigned their jobs in 2021 & 2022, turned to Freelance and gig work or opened a small business. While I strongly encourage everyone to have a "side hustle" or hobby that allows them to earn extra income, I can only wonder when employers will recognize that if allowed to take some time off work without fear of loosing their job, many employees would return refreshed or with new skills when an employer offers a Sabbatical.

This book explores two options to the Great Resignation, one for Employers (Sabbaticals) the other (Freelancing) for those considering resigning from their current job to pursue other options.

For those of you in a position to introduce real solutions to employee retention, consider offering a Bridgeway Back! As a retiree I can share the biggest obstacle many retirees with or without a Pension will face is maintaining their existing standard of living with the actual daily Cost of

Living. As inflation continues to creep upward and the possibility of a recession looming, many retirees discovered how vulnerable they were without an option to offset the increased cost of living as the price of gas and groceries soar.

Once an employee retires or leaves voluntarily, it is often difficult to return to their former employer, not for lack of skill or ability, many employers simply do not reach back. As a business and life coach I can share that many clients are "moonlighting" testing the waters on self-employment and small business ownership. There are many options and answers to the Great Resignation, Sabbaticals and Freelance are simply another option to consider.

As a former Retirement Plan Administrator, I feel our industry as a whole did a lot to improve retirement outcomes for government employees as far as securing their pensions, lower fees and greater oversight. We got a lot right yet there is more to do, building a Bridgeway Back will do more for retirees than help them maintain their standard of living, Productivity, Purpose and Pay should be a part of employee wellness. You don't know what retirement is like until you retire, and one day you may wish you did more to build a Bridgeway Back that you yourself may cross.

Sabbaticals and Freelancing are practical guides that offer a realistic insight to life after partaking in the Great Resignation or Retirement. Most clients have all the answers I simply help them find the correct questions.

Introduction to The Work Sabbatical

A sabbatical is an approved break from work, but it's not merely a fancy word for a vacation or get-away. This extended leave serves as an opportunity to continue doing work that is important and purposeful, while refreshing the body, mind, and spirit.

While on sabbatical, an individual is still employed, but is no longer required to report to work or perform any of their routine duties. Rather, during this extended leave, the individual is free to pursue other interests, such as research, furthering their education, writing, traveling, or volunteering.

The work sabbatical is most commonly recognized in educational and scientific industries, but because of its benefits, it's becoming more popular in many professions. Businesses that offer professional sabbaticals generally provide them as a benefit for employees who have worked for a specific number of years.

Depending on the company, a sabbatical may be offered as excused time off without pay, but it can also be partially or fully paid leave. The length of a sabbatical can span anywhere from 20 days to a year.

Equipped with the safety net of job security, the sabbatical is used as a time to break away from daily routines, rejuvenate, reignite inspiration, and regain clarity through a change of pace. In fact, studies show that sabbaticals result in reduced stress levels and increase an individual's productivity and satisfaction.

With so many benefits, it's no wonder why almost 25% of Fortune 500 Companies are starting to offer employee sabbaticals. Not only is it a way to retain good employees, but it also allows companies to fight burnout and nurture growth. Now, even self-employed individuals are finding ways to incorporate sabbaticals into their lives, too.

The Benefits of a Sabbatical

Although many businesses may be hesitant to offer work sabbaticals, the after-effects often benefit both the employer and employee.

#1 Employees return with new inspiration.
Regardless of how talented and loyal a long-term employee is, after working in the same job for several years, responsibilities can seem monotonous and the potential for fresh, new ideas stop. However, when that same employee is allowed a sabbatical and the security of returning to their position, there is a renewed sense of motivation.

#2 Employee creativity and excitement can benefit the employer.
Stepping away from the daily grind for an extended break can actually reignite creativity and bring about new ideas that benefit company growth.

#3 Supports a healthy work-life balance.

A dedicated employee will often put personal needs and desires on the back burner due to loyalty to their employer. While this is commendable, the most successful and resourceful employees recognize the importance of a healthy work-life balance. By offering employees the opportunity for a sabbatical, individuals can pursue things that will enrich them on a personal level, whether that is starting a side-hustle, furthering education, tending to loved one or merely taking time to mentally and emotionally reenergize. The end result is often a clearer perspective and re-prioritizing of personal and professional obligations.

#4 Promotes new opportunities for growth.

Any successful company recognizes the value and necessity of continual evolvement and by allowing more experienced employees extended time off can actually open the door for newer staff members to grow. Of course this isn't for the purpose of replacing the longtime employees, rather it creates the opportunity for cross-training among staff members. This often increases mutual respect among team members and enhances flexibility and a strong support system.

#5 Sabbaticals encourage employee loyalty.

There was a time when it was the norm for employees to remain with the same company for 20+ years. This was largely due to mutual respect between employer and employee. Such longevity was also encouraged because of 401 (k) plans and other benefits or perks awarded for multiple years of service. However, as companies began placing more importance on their bottom-line rather than valuing employees, loyalty diminished.

Nowadays, job hopping is quite common for working professionals of all ages. However, according to Harvard Business Review, the percentage of companies offering sabbaticals has increased significantly across America and many of those same companies are experiencing less employee turnover. Bottom line, it motivates new employees to reach for the goal and it shows them they are appreciated.

How a Sabbatical Can Affect Your Career

If you're not fortunate enough to work for a company that acknowledges the benefits of employee sabbaticals, there are still ways to make it happen, without it having a negative impact on your career.

The decision to take a sabbatical can be prompted by various things. Perhaps you need to care for a loved one, maybe you want to volunteer, or perhaps you feel it's time to focus on self-discovery. There's no right or wrong reason for a sabbatical, but the way you approach it with your employer is crucial.

As already established, employees are valuable resources, so before asking for the time off, carefully consider how your absence will affect the company. For example, depending on the industry, timing may be very important. Also, take into account how well-established you are with your employer. Generally, companies like Charles Schwab, Russell Investments and Clif Bar make sabbaticals available to employees every 5 or 7 years.

Another factor is the amount of time you plan to take off. Sabbaticals routinely last anywhere from 1-6 months or an entire year. Thinking through every aspect and helping to make it as seamless as possible for your employer will ensure you have a job to return to. Prior to discussing it with your employer, consider creating a detailed plan that will address potential problems and solutions.

Being completely honest about your reasons for requesting a sabbatical is also important. In addition to presenting your plan of action that prioritizes the company, it can be beneficial to arm yourself with data and statistics that will help convince your boss why this extended time off is in everyone's best interest.

Of course, being away from your job responsibilities for an extended amount of time may involve risk, depending on how well established you are. But, if you're experiencing burnout at work or feel a dire need to put personal matters first, ultimately, you are the only one who can truly know what is right for you.

Planning A Sabbatical

Taking time to properly plan a sabbatical will help ensure you make the most of your time off. Besides determining the ideal time to step away from your position, you need to establish a goal, how long your break will be, how it will be funded and how your absence will affect your career and family life.

Do your due diligence in understanding company policies on extended leave. If your employer offers sabbaticals, then all the better. However, company benefits can vary greatly. For example, determine the qualifiers such as number of years employed, how many weeks are permitted, do they offer full or partial paid-time off, will your insurance coverage continue, and so on. These factors will play a role in the planning process.

Above all, I encourage you to not give up on your dreams or innate desire to pursue a sabbatical. All too often, we prioritize careers over everything else. The motivation may stem from viewing a career as part of your identity, or financial obligations, or fulfilling expectations of others. The truth is, each of us is given a life to live.

When elderly people have been asked what they would've done differently, working harder is NEVER on the list. Rather, the most popular responses are enjoying life more and spending time with family. It's easier to regret trying something that didn't work out as planned than to never have tried.

Planning a sabbatical consists of 4 main parts:

- How will you fund your sabbatical?
- How long will you take?
- What goal do you wish to accomplish?
- What is the ideal time?

Funding Your Sabbatical

Let's face it, most of us do not enjoy discussing finances, but it's an unavoidable part of life. If you're among the lucky ones and will continue receiving a paycheck, then good for you! However, depending on the type of sabbatical you plan to take, there will likely be additional costs involved. Account for these expenses as well as your regular monthly bills so you can determine how much it will cost.

How Long Will Your Break Last?

This will be determined by the agreement made with your employer, as well as what you can realistically afford.

What Is Your Goal?

Most likely you have several ideas in mind as to what you want to do on your sabbatical. However, without having a plan in place, you risk looking back with disappointment. Also, unless you have a clear idea of what your goal is, it will be difficult to determine how much time you need and how much the endeavor will cost.

Determine the Ideal Time for a Sabbatical

There are quite a few things to consider when choosing the best time. If your sabbatical involves traveling, you'll need to consider details like weather and traveling costs. Likewise, depending on your profession, there may be certain times of the year when your employer will be more receptive to your time-off request.

Sabbatical Ideas

Perhaps you know you need some time off to recover from burnout, but aren't sure what to do. There are no right or wrong reasons for a sabbatical. However, if you need a few ideas, check these out:

- Fulfill a lifelong dream of traveling
- Personal time for rejuvenation or self-reflection
- Learn a new skill or hobby
- Start a side business

- Serve others through missionary or community volunteer work

If you've been contemplating taking extended leave from work, hopefully the information provided here has helped you decide to go for it! Life happens, desires and financial needs change, and we all need to recognize life is what we make it.

As humans we are creatures of habit. From an early age, we're taught to listen to others. First we go to school, then we get a job and have a family and daily routines and obligations are accepted, while imagination and dreams are lost. Over the years, living in auto-pilot mode caused us to forget important things in life -- living in the moment, being thankful for blessings, treating others the way we want to be treated, spending quality time with loved ones, teaching our children important life values, respect, and even self-sufficiency.

Most everyone acknowledges how the events of 2020 brought about changes. As jobs disappeared practically overnight, stores closed their doors, and people had a lot of time on their hands, many of us began reevaluating certain aspects in life. Those creative juices started flowing again, we found solutions to problems in the interest and protection of our families. New businesses were formed at an astounding rate. People searching for jobs demanded better benefits, improved work environments, and sought out companies that supported flexible schedules and a healthy work-life balance.

According to a report published in October 2021 by the U.S. Bureau of Labor Statistics, in August, 4.3 million employees quit their jobs. Reasons for these resignations included everything from refusing to deal with angry customers, finding better paying jobs elsewhere, or simply ready for a change in career. As a result, businesses are reevaluating policies to attract and keep talented, hardworking people, and fortunately offering sabbaticals is becoming more popular.

Should You Take a Sabbatical?

Successful Americans have often been viewed as workaholics, keeping their nose to the grind, working endlessly to achieve success. However, career professionals and entrepreneurs alike are beginning to see the benefits of sabbaticals.

There is a lot of benefit to stepping away from routines and focusing on something different for an extended period of time. It's as though when we become adults, we feel it's irresponsible or selfish to pursue personal interests. As a result, those dreams are pushed aside and wait until the retirement years. Well, depending on what stage of life you're in, that could be several years away. Also, as retirement age keeps being raised higher and higher, the thought of waiting can lead to frustration.

Statistics indicate that 47 is the average age that people take sabbaticals. Considering that by then, most of us have devoted 20-30 years to a career, raising a family, and approaching the empty nester years, it's logical that this stage in life will spark the desire to reevaluate things and begin searching for the ultimate work-life balance. Let's be honest, after more than two decades of being responsible, working 40+ hours weekly, and having access to a mere 2-3 week vacation each year doesn't really allow anyone to regroup or achieve a personal goal.

Be honest with yourself, how often have you said or thought - "if only I had a few months to…" Why wait? Adulthood can literally suck the life out of you if you're not careful.

Think about it: School aged kids get summer vacations, then after high-school or college graduation, many of them opt to take a "gap year" to travel, gain perspective, or do some soul searching, but once we start a career and raise a family we start to experience exhaustion and question what's next.

The once traditional formal rites of passage marking the midlife chapter included hefty pensions, retirement celebrations, and a sense of security for a leisurely future are gone. Now people are working well into their 60s and 70s, often holding jobs better suited for youthful, energetic teens, all because of insecurity and lack of purpose. Think of how much these older adults would benefit from a work sabbatical.

The life and work experience gained from people 50 and over is invaluable and having access to an extended break could serve as the launching pad to make that new stage in life personally satisfying and financially successful--for young and old.

Summary

The goal of this book is to help people from all walks of life to feel empowered and find the confidence and motivation to acknowledge desires and go after them. Whether you are employed and considering asking for a sabbatical or self-employed and strategizing how you'll juggle it, sabbaticals have been underrated for too long.

Bridgeway36 can help guide you in turning your hobby into a business. AND, if you're 50 or older, consider joining the UEO50.org newsletter to learn how you're not over the hill---you are the hill, the foundation of the future, guiding young professionals with your knowledge and experience.

The Freelancing Science

Your Step-by-Step guide to becoming a career freelancer

+an insider look at what I make (and you can too!)

"If you do what you Love you will never work a day in your life"

The question is, can doing what you Love support your lifestyle, or the lifestyle you want? Following the Covid-19 Pandemic, there was a need for businesses to implement a remote workforce which sparked the "Great Resignation". The question many faced was whether or not they would or should return to the office or find employment that allowed remote working.

The options seemed endless but the choices required a better understanding specifically, is Freelancing the same as owning a business? The answer is, kinda, not many people realize that becoming your own boss doesn't have to be synonymous with launching a business. Being your own boss can also mean being a freelancer and taking on work on a per-project basis.

As a small business owner of my own consulting "company" Bridgeway 36 Inc. I had visions of building a business for my son to run at age 36, the age he listed as his planned retirement age … when he got his first job! He is 30 years old now and has no intention of leaving the job he loves, today. As with many young adults the future is un-certain and definitely not clear.

Owning a business comes with many responsibilities and challenges but offers many benefits and rewards. I am often asked what is the difference between owning a business and freelancing? Do I have to start a business to freelance? I decided to hire a freelancer to tell her story and offer you an inside look and step by step guide to freelancing.

Table of Contents:

Chapter 1:

What in the World is Freelancing?

With the rise of the COVID-19 pandemic, the world has seen a stark rise in the number of individuals who work from home (and want to do so but haven't been able to yet).

While many of those are people whose corporate jobs allowed them the choice of staying home every day or coming into office, an entire demographic has taken it amongst themselves to change career paths and become freelancers for hire.

That said, what in the world *is* freelancing?

What is Freelancing?

Put quite simply, freelancing is a type of work where, rather than doing a specific job for a specific company at the rate of pay they provide, you do a specific set of jobs that can change as you see fit for a range of different companies and customers at rates that you set.

That probably sounded a bit confusing, so let's look at an example:

Let's say that you're a graphic designer for XYZ Corporation. Every day, you come into work at 8:00 AM because they tell you to, and you leave at 5:00 PM because they tell you to. During that workday, you complete tasks assigned to you by your manager, take your lunch when they allow you to, and deal with the customers that you are required to deal with.

Now, let's say that XYZ Corporation is shutting down and you no longer have a job. Rather than getting a position with a new company, however, you decide to become a **Freelance Graphic Designer.**

Things are a little slow at first as you learn where to find clients, what rates to charge, and how to properly pitch your services to the companies you work with, but then you read this book and it teaches you everything you need to know! You find your rhythm, and now you're a career freelancer!

So, what does your new typical work day look like?

Well, sometimes you wake up at 8AM if you feel particularly productive or have an early meeting that you've set, but most days you rise around 9:30, cook breakfast, and spend a little time appreciating the sunshine before getting to work.

Once you get to work, you choose which assignments you want to do that day while also chatting with clients about their project needs. You take on the clients you like the most, and you pitch them your rates according to what you think you should be paid for the project.

Then, you complete however much work you slated for the day from the comfort of your own home (or the office you rent). You finish up at 2pm and think about going out for the rest of the day, but then decide to do another hour of work before you do that.

So, you're out the door at 3pm with no one to tell you that you have to stay.

In a nutshell, that's what freelancing is. It's more than just managing your own schedule and charging what you think you're worth (instead of what some hotshot CEO decides you're worth).

It's freedom, and I want to give it to you.

Chapter 2:

What My World Looks Like

You're probably thinking. "*I don't really want to know what your world looks like! Just give me the info so I can get started!*"

But dear reader, you **should** see what my world looks like before you start. It's very important because freelancing isn't for everyone. There are a lot of misconceptions about what it looks like, and there are unique challenges that you'll have to face.

Let's start with the basics:

Schedule

One of the biggest reasons most people end up wanting to become freelancers is because of the freedom you have to schedule your own days. However, there are also bound to be days where you must operate on your client's timeline and you won't be able to avoid it.

Currently, I work five days a week with Saturdays and Sundays off. I do this so I can spend time with my family and fiance, as those days off line up with his. However, if you are not someone who wants weekends off, you could schedule as many or as few days off as you want, and place them wherever you like. My recommendation is that you just plan it ahead of time and stick to roughly the same schedule each week so that you can get used to how your schedule operates and advise clients on timelines accordingly.

Additionally, I don't work many hours. Each day differs, but most days I will get started on work at around 11 am and finish up at anywhere from 2 pm to 6 pm depending on a variety of factors. These factors could be anything from how much work I've scheduled myself to how many breaks I take, to how often I pick up my phone to scroll through social media (a nasty habit I need to break).

All in all, I don't work more than about 20 hours a week most weeks, which is fairly decent for my income.

Availability

In the freelancing world, schedule and availability are very similar, but I consider by schedule to be the times when I am actually working and my availability to be the hours of the day where I am available to chat with clients.

Generally, I am available for clients all day every day, so long as I am awake and not at any special event. If I were to go to a baby shower or wedding, for example, I would turn my phone off and respond to my clients once I had left.

Additionally, your clients generally expect you to be available when they need you. For me, this means that I can end up on Zoom calls or texting clients as late as 11 pm at night depending on what country they are in.

To me, this is the biggest downfall of freelancing. It has been the thing I struggle with the most, simply because it feels like I am never truly "off work." Don't get me wrong, I get plenty of time off—it just doesn't feel that way because of how frequently I have to spend time talking to and updating my clients.

Key Struggles

Just about everyone knows the good parts of freelancing. What most experts won't tell you, however, is what the bad parts are. I consider myself a transparent person, though, and I would hate for you to waste your time pursuing something that won't make you happy in the end. So, I'm not holding back.

Here is my list of key struggles that I have faced in becoming a freelancer:
- Self-management and waking up at a decent hour (after a while, your sleep schedule is bound to get messed up if you aren't on a very strict bedtime).
- Lack of work in the beginning (when you're new, it's difficult to get clients because you lack very much freelancing experience).
- What I call "lulls" in business—times of the year when your orders suddenly and

drastically decrease for what seems like no reason at all. However, it always picks back up within a few weeks and it's very been so slow that I couldn't pay my bills.

- Maintaining a healthy deity and exercise regime (I'm always at my desk)
- Feeling trapped in my home because of how many hours I spend in my home office, typing away.

These are not all of the struggles I face by a long shot, but it should effectively demonstrate to you that freelancing does not come without its fair share of hardships—nor should you expect it to.

Income

Drum roll please It's the moment you've been waiting for!

I don't know about you, but before I started freelancing, I wanted to see real, hard and fast numbers. I wanted to know what my earning potential was and what lows I could expect as well. And who wouldn't?! That's the safe thing to do!

Unfortunately, however, most freelancers are less thank transparent about what they actually make, and most numbers you see are either pre-tax, over-exaggerated, or both.

Here's what I actually make as someone who has been a freelance writer for less than one year, broken down:

Monthly:

Monthly, I can expect to make anywhere between $2,000 and $6,000, depending on my level of business and how much I push myself. However, keep in mind those taxes. For a freelancer who owns her own LLC, I'm taxed the same as a sole proprietorship.

Normally, when you work with a corporation, you actually only pay half of your taxes. The business employing you pays the other half. With sole proprietorships (and single-owner LLCs) however, you are responsible for paying both the employer and the employee portion.

Most people are taxed at an average of 15% in the United States where I live, which means I am responsible for taking 30% out for taxes each time I pay myself.

So, those numbers look very different once you do the math.

That $2,000 becomes $1,400 and that $6,000 becomes $4,200.

It really doesn't seem fair, does it?

But, unfortunately, this is the way things must work.

Yearly

So, with such a large variance, what does my yearly income end up at?

Well, that's quite difficult to say, as it changes from year to year.

In 2021, I began freelancing in February, so you have to account for all the time I was building my business and charging outrageously low prices. After all was said and done, though, my income came out to just under $30,000 for my freelancing alone.

Another thing to keep in mind, though, is that as a freelancer, you have much more time to pursue side incomes and passive income opportunities. You can work effectively on selling digital downloads and being an affiliate marketer, which is where the bulk of most freelancers' incomes come from!

Once you add the income I made from my side hustles (which I do almost no work on myself now because it runs itself), I did much better and landed close to $40,000 after taxes.

This year, because I'm starting with higher prices and my side incomes are already established, I'm expecting a bit more than that.

So, with all this in mind, do you still want to become a freelancer?

If not, feel free to put this book down, because the rest of it won't serve you any good.

If you are still chasing the dream, however, read on. I have some very valuable information to share with you.

Chapter 3:

Step-by-Step Guide to Freelancing

Ah, you're still with me! Good, I'm glad. I was afraid I might have scared you off with all my doom and gloom talk.

But it's true, freelancing isn't easy all the time, and it isn't anywhere near as easy as most of your influencers will make it out to be. So I like to make it clear what you're getting yourself into before you actually get into it. After all, I would hate to waste your time.

That said, let's jump straight into how to get started as a freelancer, step-by-step.

Step 1: Setup

As with anything, you're going to need to set yourself up before you actually jump in headfirst. Setup is perhaps the most important part of the process, so make sure you don't neglect it in your excitement to get started.

Now, the easiest (and the quickest) way to get started as a freelancer is to begin on a freelance website.

Personally, I advise you not to stay on the freelancing sites forever because they have a habit of selling your skills short and make people think that you're worth far less than you are, but as a beginner who needs some experience, it's a valuable platform.

Right now, the top two freelancing platforms are Fiverr and Upwork, and you can choose either or both to set up your first profile on. For reference, Fiverr allows buyers to come to you and place their orders through a gig system (which means you may get orders you don't want, as you don't have the option to decline them until after they are placed) and Upwork has a system where you bid for jobs using Connects. With Upwork, you have a little more say over what you do and I believe the commission Upwork takes from you is a little less, but the Connects you receive are limited per month. Once you run out, you have to either wait for your refresher or buy more.

With that said, it's always a good idea to set up both in the beginning so you can find which one works best for you. For me, it was Fiverr. For you, it could be Upwork. You never know until you get started.

Now, as you're setting up your profile, pay special attention to the bio box, as people will read it a lot. I've actually had clients message me and tell me they wanted to work with me on the sole basis of loving the bio I have. **It's *that* important.**

Additionally, decide what your rates will be and what will be included in your packages. For example, if you want to write ebooks for people, decide if you'll also be doing covers, formatting, etc, or if you'll charge extra for those. Alternatively, you may choose not to offer them at all and stick to just the writing. There's nothing wrong with that, but you may lose a few clients because of it.

Once you've got your profiles set up, move on to the next step!

Step 2: Customer Acquisition

The first customer you get as a freelancer will always be the hardest, as well as the most important. It's the one that gives you hope and validation, as well as the one that tells you what methods of yours are working versus what isn't. It's also the one that will kick your freelancer profile into the algorithm so that you can start getting more orders on a regular basis. On Fiverr especially, getting one client will quickly lead to a cascade of others.

To get that first customer, you're going to have to really get out of your comfort zone. You'll have to try different proposal types if you're on Upwork and bid for Buyer Requests if you're on Fiverr.

If you want your first customer as quickly as possible, however, I recommend doing neither.

That's right, neither.

Instead, head over to some freelancing Facebook groups. Other freelancers outsource to these groups all the time, which means you'll have the chance to bid on jobs where you can introduce yourself to the buyer personally, build a reputation within the group, and (if you're quick enough) be the very first to apply.

In my experience, the best group for doing this is a Facebook group called Freelancing Mentorship with Alexandra Fasulo. Many of the freelancers in this group started out just like you, so they're very sympathetic with your plight. Because of this, it will be much easier to get that first client.

My advice is to get on that group, and look for jobs as soon as your profile is set up! Once you've done that and gotten your first review, customers will begin pouring in.

Step 3: Outsourcing

As you continue to gain clients, some of which are even regulars, you will eventually find yourself at a bottleneck where you want to make more money but simply don't have the capacity to take on any more work. When this happens, I implore you to consider outsourcing.

Outsourcing is essentially where you pay another freelancer to do the work you've been hired to do for a lesser price than what you're being paid. This way, the freelancer gets the majority cut for the work they've done and you still get paid your share as a sort of finder's fee. After all, that person wouldn't have that job if it weren't for you!

Now, before it comes up, this practice is widely accepted in the world of freelancing and is completely ethical. In fact, most freelancers you outsource to will assume that you're making something off the deal—otherwise, there's no point in you having taken it!

I do recommend though that you don't tell them exactly how much you're making, unless you want them to ask for more money. It's just standard practice to keep that information to yourself—nothing good ever comes out of it when you don't.

Eventually, once you're at this long enough, you may also consider starting your own agency where you hire writers and do virtually none of it yourself! This happens very far down the road for most freelancers (if at all) but it is definitely something to shoot for if that sounds like a goal you like.

Final Advice

Now that we've reached the end of this ebook, there isn't much left for me to say, other than that I wish you luck. Freelancing is one of those jobs that can make you want to rip your hair out but that is also so rewarding.

Now, most people will tell you not to give up no matter what, but I think that's awful advice.

So, here's mine:

If you give up, give up for the right reasons.

If you decide that freelancing just isn't for you, or that you struggle too much with managing yourself, or that you simply don't like some aspect of it that you hadn't considered before, then those are all valid reasons for you to call it quits. After all, there's no point in being a freelancer if it doesn't make you happy. Heck, there's no point in doing anything if it doesn't make you happy.

If the reason you're giving up though is something like struggling to acquire clients or fear of failure, then I urge you to keep going. Try it out for one more week, and then do another. If you love it, then you **will** find a way to make it work.

The only freelancers that fail are those that give up and refuse to learn.

So long as you aren't one of them, your success is guaranteed.

www.ingramcontent.com/pod-product-compliance
Lightning Source LLC
Chambersburg PA
CBHW071112220526

45467CB00004B/1835